EDOH STEPHEN OWOICHO

Woman of Honour

This book was professionally typeset on Reedsy.
Find out more at reedsy.com

Dedicated to all those who lost their lives in the pursuit of equity and peace in this turbulent world.

Contents

Preface

I remember sitting on the sofa when a voice reached out to me with a message from the Frontiers of Zion revealing, " The hour has come for you to begin the translation of the end-time revival through the influence of the quickened words I will place beneath thy fingertips." Indeed, it was a feeling that gave birth to a delightful aura. I didn't need anybody at that moment to inform me about the presence of the Holy Spirit.

I warmly received the glorious message He came to deliver. It's was all about a mandate that will kick me into the limelight but all for God's glory that will profit the denizens of the Earth and bring them closer to Jesus Christ.

The year 2019 was a year of encounters. I could recall desiring for an encounter that will stamp my vision as God's pioneered one. I wanted the same kind of experience the Biblical prophet Samuel had to replicate in my life. As though, I felt maybe I was kidding but I wasn't! He came in various forms, most especially in the faces of patriarch and Generals of the face; laying hands on my hands as a sign of impartation. Indeed, it was a lovely experience.

The message that came forth arrived with an instruction to put forth three books. I was confused because I have no formal experience. But

He gave me assurance that He would uphold and show me the things I knoweth not. Of course, He did as He proposed. God is really nice.

The book, "A New Dawn" came forth as the first book out of the three God proposed. It came along with powerful connotations that will espouse the total annihilation of failure and fear, and too give hope to the feeble. It's isn't a book that translates from a fictional tale or personal imagination. No! It was birth forth from the throne room of Heaven.

Soon after, "I Am Different" arrived with the purpose of transforming Christians especially the youths into the original entities God created. I have to bring this to your remembrance; in the last day's young men shall prophesy, old men shall dream dreams, your maidservants shall see visions, etc. Today, if you take a survey or perhaps an analytical test on those who are functioning in their original calling, you will found out that only 10 per cent out of the millions of youths around the world are effectively translating the rhyme of Zion in their lives. For this reason, the book "I Am Different" came forward.

Finally, the glorious Celestial king grants me the over warm privilege of translating the tunes of Zion to the feminists around the entire mortal realm by birthing forth the book titled, " Woman of Honour." This is a book for every feminist; Women, ladies, and every girl child.

Feminism is a culture of the Zionist tribe. In the city of Zion, certain translations take effect that aims for the transformation of every woman, lady, and the girl child.

Honour is an impression that arose from certain key factors that will be collected related to you as you embark on your new to the doorway of honour. Cheers!

Edoh Stephen woicho.

Lead Pioneer, Words Citadel Family.

Acknowledgement

I'm grateful to everyone who made sure I was in good health in the course of putting together this great book.

I want to say a big thank you. And God bless you.

Difference

Many years ago, after claiming an accolade for the best student in Science, I exclaim a saying within that moment; I'm different! Yeah, I wouldn't doubt the fact I was then.

Life sometimes seems different, but we are the one to make it a difference. It's quite an amazing experience, each time I walked down the street, only to be put to notice the various characters and features exhibited by some people.

The term "Difference" as defined by Merriam Webster's dictionary, is the quality that distinguishes an individual or a thing from another. Everything: [Living and None living thing] on earth possess a difference in its various aspects; character, manner of approach, culture, etc.

Just as the title of this chapter implies different, we will emphasise more on the term "difference" in this series. What kind of difference are we about to speak on? A positive one!

I grew up successfully in the satellite-village of Karu, Nasarawa State, Nigeria, with no negative record found in my history. This was a place where cultists, gamblers, smokers, etc., lives and operate at a higher frequency. But how did I cope with those folks? I embraced a difference back then, as a callow lad. I am privileged to be raised in a disciplined home, where I was nurtured to differentiate the good from the bad, also was cautioned against involving in negative errands. Today, I thank my parent for nurturing me in the right ordeal. It pays to adhere to good counsel.

A difference makes an individual unique, elegant, patented and peculiar. Great Men like W.F. Kumuyi, Ben Carson, Bill Gates, Aliko Dangote, Mark Zuckerberg, Cristiano Ronaldo, David Oyedepo, Tb Joshua, etc., are where they are today because they embraced a difference.

The reason we have a failed generation is that we haven't accepted a difference! Stealing today has become rampant in the universe. You could visualise this feature—stealing, in the life of most youths in our society. Unfortunately, only a few haves been youths with a difference. Failure to embrace a positive change could destabilise an individual, society, and the nation.

"Greatness starts by accepting a difference," — Stephen Edoh

Now walk with me, as we both step into the affirmation train, where I shall speak more on this chapter.

THE SIGHTFUL YOU

"When you are sightful, you're a victor," –Stephen Edoh

He has to learn to soar higher to a greater altitude than the other birds. What a hardworking, vibrant, fearless, agile, and sightful creature, He is!

The features; speed, agility, tenacity, etc. He possesses claims Him an accolade for an astonishing display of flightmanship. We call Him The Eagle!

A long time ago, something happened; Our resident home key got missing, leaving us with no option than to remain outside, till we think on the next line of action. On everyone's face, you could observe a poor sense of being. Having searched the key for hours, others sat down because of fatigue. But with me, it was the opposite. I begin the search again; I was confident in myself and also; I was optimistic that I will find the key. It went in my favour; I found the key!

The worst experiences a man could have is having sight without vision and courage. I feel for the blind because they too want to see, work and live happily. But the unfortunate thing is this; some individual has sight, but they aren't bringing the best it of it. A sightless fellow has nothing to offer to His or Her family and their society. But here comes a sightful, skilled and vibrant person, etc. who enjoys the benefit of being sighting.

Just as the Super-Eagle was in the movie, titled: Angry Birds, I encourage you to be a replica with a difference, because it rewards to be sightful. I know you're enjoying the journey, stay calm with me as we continue our conversation in this affirmation train.

THE BRAINIAC–YOU

"You are what you are now; genius, dummy, star, mediocre, etc.: because of what you say concerning yourself," — Stephen Edoh

When God created man, he didn't place him on an equal level with the animals, rather he placed man above. We are the set of mammals designed to be accurate, smart, discerning, and great. Unlike animals! Unfortunately, many have failed to realise that God created them to operate at a higher frequency. Note this; We were all created with an intelligence feature endowed in us. None was left behind when God was creating the universe. He gave us all equal ability. It's just that many do not understand who they are. This scenario has led many to affirm the fact that God created some people to be special, but this isn't true. God created us all equally!

The Brainiac you is the accurate you, the intelligent you, also the fast and spontaneous you. Everyone needs to understand this; an individual must possess a unique feature before he or she can take over the world. The talk of intelligence is fundamental. You re a genius, an icon, a star and all of a protagonist. It has to come to your awareness that you're the person as mentioned above. When I say I'm a factor of honour and am isn't using my six-senses as required of me, then I'm a hypocrite! You are intelligent, yes that's true, but it isn't enough. You still have to be creative, that's why this series nicknamed you; The Brainiac!

Your knowledge has to be espoused by creativity to birth out an effective result. Life must be ruled by intelligence and assisted by creativity. Take, for example, Dr Benjamin Carson, who engaged his experience concerning the snooker game to a complicated situation where hope was lost, and hope was restored. What kind of complicated situation did he encounter? A medical one; Congenitally joined-babies brought forth for a surgical operation. Think of this; what if Dr Ben has refused to apply that experience? The Congenitally united-twins would have been at the grave by now. But thank God, it was the opposite!

The same way you mix primary colours just to end up with several beautiful colours, the same should go with your six senses. Therefore,

I urge you to add creativity to whatever you're doing to bring forth an excellent result.

Stay with me, as the journey continues.

UNDERSTANDING THE MYSTERY OF THE DIFFERENT YOU

"Only the different you yould take the world," –Stephen Edoh

We live in a time where individuals succeed, only when they possess a difference. Gone are the days of helping hands, liberators, philanthropist, etc. Our generation has failed to concord with the fact that; a difference is all we need to succesuchnd move the world to the next level.

The mystery of the different you are a series that has been put in place, to unveil you into the hall of honour.

We are all aware that life is full of mysteries, strategies, rules, principles, formulas, etc. For us to put any vision into execution, we must know and understand a mystery. I have put a mystery in place, and I call it, "the mystery of the different you."

Earlier in this series, we could explore two vital horizons, but as our journey in the affirmation train continues, let us go explore!

YOUR VALUE AND WORTH

"The recipe to mostt of our common failures birth into existence, the moment we realised our worth and value." -Stephen Edoh.

However, the dual terms; (worth and value) are both synonymous.

5

Therefore, we shall use the word 'worth' in this series. Worth as defined by the Merriam Webster's dictionary entails the monetary or material value of something.

Understanding how much your worth as a woman is your key to exploitation. Remember, you are worth more than silver, gold, rubies, and diamond. You don't need anyone to tell you how much you worth, all I know is this; you worth something bigger! Unfortunately, mediocrity and indifference have overshadowed our world. Today, we could find individuals who just feel inferior, with no vision and aspiration. In case you're one, don't panic, I have put in this book placed for your sake.

So many years ago, on a certain night, Mr Johnson got robbed; He loosed all his valuable properties to the robbers who invaded his house. Quite an unfortunate scenario. We found MR Johnson crying, someone asked him a question, Why are you crying? MR Johnson replied The properties I lost to the rubbers are worth's millions of dollars'. What a tragedy!

Now, I want you to see your life in terms of value, as those properties that were robbed off Mr Johnson. You don't have to bring down yourself, because someone mocked your dressing, home, grammar, No! You are different with a difference. Have it in your six senses you are!

I discover this over the years, influence and challenges now seem to be a disaster to youths, rather than motivation in this generation. How do I mean? Go to certain homes, campuses, streets, etc., You will come to realise how some ladies and even women in need of wants, becomes influenced negatively by their friends.

Unfortunately, because of the words their friends used in challenging them, they make decisions tthet end up ruining their entire life; going into negative acts such as adultery, prostitution just to makes ends meets.

Never subjugate yourself to any err voice, flee from any conversation that does not connote positivism or holiness. You're whom God says you're, not what they say you're. Yet, they might insult you, just keep calm, because your status is changing soon, there is no more decline, all that should be your thought is this; I'm on my way to a better day.

Trust yourself, put a smile on your face and say this to the air; I'm the best and none is better than me!

YOUR IDENTITY

"I've always believed myself, and the place I came from and the place I'm going to," – Stephen Edoh

A woman's personality is her Prestige.

When an individual confesses, "I am different, he or she must possess the capacity to understand his or her identity.

Life without identity is the same as sight without vision. I affirm the fact that your identity is your pride. Many have failed because they lack knowledge about their identity.

Identity is the qualities, beliefs, etc., that make a particular woman or group unique from others. When a lady or a woman understand the difference she possessed, she wouldn't be mocked, downcast, insulted, etc., because something is speaking on her behalf and identity!

The reason most people don't know their worth is that they lacked an identity of who they truly are. When you learn to see yourself a different way from others, your life brings forth the original result of your identity. Hear this, God created no one to be inferior, but superior. The only difference between the rich and the poor is knowledge. Your journey to success starts now. A different being is now in you, not the old person you used to be. But how, Mr Steve? Because when you come to know and understand your identity, you, therefore, stepped out of mediocrity to the path of a positive difference!

The thought you had as of last night was the former. Therefore, you've to skip it, advance and work on yourself. Think of this, Google play store sent updating messages concerning applications installed on your phone. But why these messages keep coming? So you can upgrade to the latest version, because at any point we experience a change, an unusual aura is unveiled.

So, what was I trying to saying in the previous paragraph? You must change your old style to a recent one, in all aspect; character, beliefs, way of life, etc.

Remember, it's your identity that reviews the qualities you possess, the belief you summit too, and the rules you concord to.

Stay cool!!

Key nuggets of this chapter

· A difference makes an individual unique, elegant, patented and peculiar.

· Your knowledge has to be espoused by creativity to birth out an effective result

· The mystery of the different you are a series that has been put in place, to unveil and open you up to an additional dimension.

· Never subjugate yourself to any err voice, flee from any conversation that does not connote positivism or holiness.· Identity is the qualities, beliefs, etc., that make a particular person or group different from others.

· The reason most people don't know their worth is that they lacked an identity of who they truly are.

Keep calm, we have just left a very important phase. I know you are enjoying the journey, place a amile on our face, as we continue our conversation in this affirmation train.

Boom!!!!!!!!!!!!!!!!!!!!!!

We believe that this very chapter has blessed you. It will be an honour to be of good counsel to you. More so, it would be more pleasurable to receive help from you.

Stephen Edoh Ministries and Words Citadel Family needs your partnership to continue to spread God's words via writing to the nations.

We need your support. It could be monthly remittance, perhaps just a moment's help.

Further, we are available to help you with good counsel, and words of Hope that will brings about restoration in all aspects of life.

Remember, that we are your friends and you can reach out to us with the email below.

Indeed, there is no price tag for every counsel offered. It is free of charge.

You can send your partnership or one-time support payment through our PayPal email address below.

You can also testify to how this book has impacted your life using the same email below.

We love and care for you.

PayPal payment email address: **Stephenedoh2000@gmail.com**

Pay Pal link: **www.Paypal.me/StephenEdoh**

Thank you and many blessings to you and your family.

Intentionality

"Intentional ladies are mighty entities from the frontier of Zion."
— Stephen Edoh.

The phrase "intentionality" is conceived from the noun, "intention" and the added suffix, "-lity." It defines an attitude that conveys the newness of life and that which features connote the manifestations and approaches of the Celestial father in the earth realm. Intentionality is the language of the elite tribe and the remnants of the altruistic part of the mortal realm. It isn't a character virtue for a specific gender difference. No! It's a virtue that everyone cleaned off sin, is to be proud of emulating.

Every intentional lady and woman is an explicit description of honour. Intentionality is a melody played from the horizon of Zion in the life of every lady or woman whose aura is defined by honour. It is the dimension of God's module of Operandi; a portal that triggers the momentum of persistence, determination, striving, etc., in the life of every living matter.

The dimensions of God module of Operandi singly open to those who are ready to submit to the will and sovereignty of the one and only supreme

God. Intentionality is the model of every lady and woman of honour. It is the difference between the active and passive pair of humans. It distinguishes a lady to be active; when she is competitive, strong, healthy, enthusiastic, etc. Otherwise, she's passive and mundane.

Intentionality is a prototype that birth the trailblazing impulse in the life of every purpose-driven lady, woman, or girl child. It's coordinate the journey of greatness; also birth forth the courage in the life of a lady or a woman to withstand the travails of life. When a lady or a woman lacks the vibes of intentionality, she keeps the house in the state of intricacy.

Life is an anecdote that is illustrated at the reason of time; its effect, understanding, and management. In the tale of existence, there isn't a free space to counterfeit or mess up on the journey to becoming a woman of honour. Therefore, every lady must act so intentionally because she's a plotter of ideas, an oracle of love, a pioneer of success, a missionary from the city of Zion, of all, an epistle of God grace.

A PLOTTER OF IDEAS

"Every lady and woman of honour is a plotter of ideas,"—Stephen Edoh.

Who is a plotter of ideas? An intentional woman!

The Earth in its interminable survival journey has experienced several moves that have brought it this far from the dark phase to its present phase. In the early age, when the earth still dwells in the dark phase; it was at the advent stage of civilization. Unfortunately, in the advent phase of civilization, women were glimpsed as custodians of homes and entities that pioneers reproduction. However, in these last days, women are now seen as mighty vessels and trailblazers of age.

A plotter of ideas isn't a formulator of negative suggestions but an inventor of solutions to the many World problems we can mention of today. Earlier in this series, I asked a question, who is a plotter of ideas? And then, a direct answer came forth; An intentional Woman!

Ine criterion that defines a woman of Honour is her ability to plot ideas that translate for the interest of all and not just her family alone.

We live in a time when the preponderance of the world population are looking up to you as a therapy to their problems. The Bible book of Isaiah in its chapter 61 vs 1 down to 3, give clear emphasis on the fact of intentionality; how you were called to mend the broken-hearted, to grant liberty to the captives, etc.

You know what? You can't afford to leave them in the lurch, because deep in you settled a river of working ideas, solutions, and a healing balm.

Rise, darling! It's time you go out and prove to the world you are an antidote to her problem; in your hands is inserted a healing balm meant for her injury; in your mouth live words flavoured with the fragrance of serenity; in your mind settled an ocean of clues that will take the world to the phase of radiant splendour.

Don't help push the people to their extinction, rather be you sent on a mission; one sent to serve brings about peace, and too, convey happiness in other to establish an evergreen World.

A MISSIONARY

"In the Biblical era, there were only a few women who pioneered various moves such as Deborah, Esther, Priscilla, Anna, Ruth, Naomi, Mary,., but in this age, we have experienced the good works of the countless female missionaries that served in time; both the ones who are late and the ones who are still alive," —Stephen Edoh

Modernisation is an experience that advent from the impact of the missionary journey that took place in the life of the early missionaries such as John Wesley, George Whitfield, Charles Wesley, Maria Wood-worth—Etter, Kathryn Kuhlman, William Tyndale.

Aside from the missionaries, there were several territorial subjugators who after bringing a country to her downfall brought forth a new style and culture to their new subdued colony. An excellent example includes men such as Júlio César, Alexander the Great, and the ancient Babylonia custodians.

Every generation or era has a record of men that subjugated territories and lesser authorities. The above nobles mentioned weren't men that subjugate for slavery, sex, or one other reason we don't really know.

In the evolution cycle of civilization, unorthodox moves took effect. Some mighty men of took conquest in their subdued nations; compelling them to their decree. While some others subjugate to remodel, transform and to innovate the mind-set of the citizens of the subdued province. Women of honour are a team of persons missions define whose way of life. Every woman of honour is a true missionary! In these last days, they are none willing to leave the tale of existence without fulfilling the undertaking he or she was sent here on Earth to fulfil. Until we all realised that we are here on a mission to fulfil an undertaking and not our own wishes, we stride on the hallway to complications.

When a woman realised her mission on Earth, her life translates on the path of delight. She becomes a factor of celebration to her generation. The one unfortunate thing is this; most people out there will call you names because of jealousy and envy, but you have to give no ears. You are here on Earth for a mission to be fulfilled. It's never too early or too late to work on your reasons for being on the surface of the earth. The only thing that can stop you is your mindset.

AN ORACLE OF LOVE

"Every certified lady or woman of honour is an oracle of love."—Stephen Edoh.

Love is an action word that modifies the positive thoughts and affections an individual has toward another individual or a thing of nature. It's not just an affection modifier, it is the centre focal point of a heart-driven and espoused by altruism. In the absence of love, thoughts of evil supersede over the heart of a man on every aspect; governance, attitude, etc.

Today, many don't understand the meaning of the word, 'love.' With some, it is the character identity that demands you treat your husband or devotee modestly and acceptably. Yes, it is true, but it is beyond that! Love is not a display of an action that positively affect the life of a single person but groups of teams of persons out there; it could be a community, or the nations of the world.

Who is an Oracle of love? One who understanding the coding and translations that spring forth the resultant effect of altruism in the tale of mankind. Oracle's of love are those set of individuals who act and function as a translator of love, also engineers the spirit of smiling in the life of many outs there by the coding and processing of various positive deeds into their doings.

In a world where men struggle to survive, only love can redeem it. The act of expressing love is the ordinance of liberating the joy of multiple people out there. When the fragrance of love is released into an environment, the aura experienced a shift in all levels of human endeavour.

Men such as Nelson Mandela fought for his nation's freedom because of the love he has for them. Think of this, was he the only man in entire South Africa? No, but something led him to engage in that quest for liberation, and it is the spirit of love. When love takes over a territory, unity becomes an actuality, and poverty comes to be a yore tale.

When you confront a woman love distinguishes whose lifestyle, you've encountered an entity whose heart's molecular structure portrays an outlook of a decent aura. Love is not just an action or a doing. It is the language of men and women whose life conveys the doings and methodology of the Celestial King. Until women of love arise, the preponderance of the countless homes around the world suffers inflammations and drawbacks.

Love doesn't boast for itself, the Bible told us so. It's a vessel that carries everyone along. It conveys an expression that connotes care, interest, respect, etc. When love leads, peace, unity, and progress become the motto of an individual, some group of persons, and a nation.

Feminism without love expresses negativism. As a lady or woman of valour, your life must replicate the lifestyle of an envoy whose life inscribed, emit, and surface love. Women of honour are entities of genuine conscience. When your conscience is cleaned of pride and envy, you then carry others along with your boat. But an exception to this negligence becomes the resultant effect of your character.

Remember, love is the greatest of all ideas, things, thoughts in the tale of mankind. It pays to love. God is a friend of those whose life emit the rays of love to others. In the days of trouble and trails, He stands as an advocate for them. The one most impressing thing about love is this, it does not a witch hunt the expressing vessel. But it differs with the wicked. Their act of evil witch hunts them later in the series of life.

I'll be glad if you become an oracle, or perhaps an envoy of love, this day. Many people out there refused to give aids to the poor and their ignores community because of fear of being killed, attacked, etc. But the factual justification of this cliché stands firm. It isn't a fiasco!

None has the power, authority, permission, and approval to exterminate you when the Celestial father hasn't approved of it. Yet, you might be attacked, but He is with you right where you are. One fascinating thing I can tell you about love is this, "the act of conveying love is a unique prayer that outclassed the reasons for and effects of normal prayer."

God is not looking for people who will articulate love for the purpose of seeking relevance and attention. No! He is looking for men willing to convey, translates, and overshadowed the entire earth realm with the Fragrance of love. Let me recall you of something to note, and never should you skipped it out of your mind; the envoys of love are kingdom remnants.

Who are the kingdom Remnants? These are custodians of God's manifestations in the mortal realm. Fortunately, you are a kingdom remnant because you convey the greatest of all messages from the realm of glory: a place that housed innumerable companies of angels and the host of other entities.

Stay with me!

Culture

"**O**nly the culture you acknowledged helps to prevail over your adversity,"—Stephen Edoh.

The word "Culture" originates from a Latin word—cultura; it means beliefs, custom, standard, similarly, it is synonymous with the word "Civilization". Culture is as old as a man.

Every individual on the surface of the Earth belowngs to a particular unit that shares the same ideology, methodology and the same beliefs system.

Culture is an abstract stuff of nature that defines uniqueness, difference, cooperation, and unionism. It brings a set of people together, also; it promotes unity and peaceful Co-existent. The essence of culture cannot be further articulated because it is as old as man. For now, we will only refer to culture as the way of life of a particular group of people.

When you read through the principle of taxonomy that was proposed by the great Carl Linnaeus as of old, you will agree with me that there are several dimensions in the hierarchy of life, and every living organism found in the various dimensions has a culture they cultivate to acclimatise and adapt to the conditions in its domain.

Come with me to the kingdom Animalia; an empire that housed several animals amongst others. In this kingdom, every animal has its style or way of life. Take, for example, the culture, or way of life of the blue-green algae differs from that of the Nematode; tapeworm. So do the same with the Tiger and the domestic Goat.

Every woman is a key factor, component, and end product of creation. The Bible refers to the woman as a help-meet; nojustust to her husband as the Bible writer implies, but to a community, country, and of all, a generation.

"Women are beyond help meets, they are the treasure that worth more than rubies, diamond and gold." —Stephen Edoh.

A woman of honour is a woman of culture! She's a unique personage from the throne room of heaven, a platter of ideas, an oracle of love, and a mother to nations. In the absence of a culture, a woman is no longer a mother but an odd prototype.

Don't sense this moment to be a coincidence, but accept it as a moment that the Divine Father has translated from Zion into reality. Walk with me. As our journey to greatness, starts with only a few steps.

Women and Civilization

"Women are weapons and vital tools to developing the entire universe and espousing it to the phase of radiant splendour." – Stephen Edoh.

We refer to civilization as a thing as of old in its initial stage. It is the bedrock of modernisation, secularism, atheism, science, and many much more. In the cradle of civilization, we knew women to be house stewards and commodities that pioneers reproduction.

However, in the latter phase of civilization, we now view women as a vibrant force; stronger than the dual-nuclear forces; electromagnetic and gravitational force. Her ideas now translate into solutions to world problems.

Civilization has inflicted a lot in the heart of people resulting in the birth of several negative occurrences that are affecting the Earth flora and fauna. Unfortunately, women are victims of this negative circumstance. In a clear transition, they are turning out to become a dynamo pioneering the whirlwind of civilization. But it differs with you reading this book because you are a woman of honour, dignity, and good morals.

Until this period in the cycle of evolution, many women started several tremendous actions such as Mother Teresa, Kathryn Kuhlman, Pandita Ramabai, Mary Slessor, Dora Akunyili, and many much more. One most shocking thing is this; many ladies and girls in this generation want to be like the above nobles, but they lack a true culture!

Nowadays, every woman of honour has a culture, and her culture is her equivalence, personality, essence, beauty, colour, and charisma. For you to succeed in the jet age, you must cultivate a style of life that detail positivism. We live in a time when many ladies toil, all because they didn't acknowledge the fact that only culture can destroy the whirlwind of civilization.

Many ladies are on the street, day after day roaming about like scalar quantities, all because a platform isn't there. But the fact is this; as a woman of honour, you are the perfect description of success, an authentic platform, because you adopted a culture. I've to say this; if at any stage you have completely submitted to the impetuses and forces of civilization, I think it's time you withdraw because it won't take you anywhere but shortens your journey in the tale of existence.

Stay with me!

The True Culture

"There isn't any free space for counterfeiting in the route that leads one to success, only a true culture guides one through." –Stephen Edoh.

True culture is not a sweet-cake fantasy to overlook if we sideline the fact of paying a price. We live in a time and season when the preponderance of masses acts so crazy that got me thinking if life worth living to some folks. The true and positive impact of civilization on the Earth flora and fauna birthed from nothing but a true culture.

Every Nation exploiting today are being aided and pioneered by a true culture. The reason Africa and Her nations are still backward in the technological and economical phase of civilization is that Her leaders lack a true culture. Unfortunately, the kickoff of civilization undertook in Africa.

I once asked myself this question, why do many ladies suffer early divorce after marriage in this generation? But then a thought roams through my mind, this was it; virtue and usefulness are absent in the life of most individuals in this generation, especially with the ladies. This is true! Nowadays, most ladies seem to act awkwardly and dance to the whirlwind of civilization all in the name of trends.

The true culture of Feminism is not established in the usefulness of technological devices, but two things; purpose and love. Most ladies as earlier said are dancing awkwardly to the rhythm of civilization, instead of aligning to the tune of purpose and love. Any lady who is purpose-driven and influenced by love soar higher to the hilltop of life.

Love and value are the two essential features to be noted when discussing a true culture. The term "love" make a woman unique, exciting, and precious. It does not boast or act proud. It makes one humble. In the omission of love, a woman of honour becomes a mundane woman.

The wine of genuine love is sweeter than that made from the grapefruit. When a woman operates in love, she prom in the rhythm of peace, joy, and harmony. Love is beyond a tale of favour, joy, kindness, and care, it's a mystery! Until you translate on the tune of love, your life will keep experiencing unfavourable circumstances.

We live in a time when the whirlwind of civilization is waging a war against the rhythm of the end-time revival. Today, purpose is sidelined from the thoughts of youths and a lot of matured individuals out there. Unfortunately, the devil pioneers these all! It hurt me seeing many people ruining the undeserving privilege of breath.

Every woman of honour is a subject of purpose. It's with time, a woman discovers her mission on Earth. No one entity on Earth is purposeless, no! We are all here (Earth) on an assignment under the directorate of Zion. If, as a lady, you are yet to discover your purpose, don't panic if perhaps you once panicked, this book is here to align with you.

Keep calm as we advance.

How to discover the woman of honour in you:

1.Accept Jesus Christ as your Lord and Saviour.

2.Develop a delightful relationship with the celestial sovereignty.

3.Align your life to the will of the Jesus and subject your under life under the directorate of the Divine Spirit; the holy spirit. This Is the axis, you will come to discover your reasons for being on Earth.

4.Live a life that detail positivism.

Summary

1.A woman of honour is a woman of a genuine culture.

2.She's a trailblazer to a civilised world.

3.She's a mother and not a model.

4.She's the perfect description of love.

5.She's a woman of purpose.

6.She's a true feminist.

7.She's a missionary from Zion.

8.She's a vibrant force that subdues the whirlwind of civilization.

9.She's a Godly woman.

Identity

"**Y**our identity is a clear picture of your past, present, and even your future– if a change doesn't translate." –Stephen Edoh.

The morpheme "Identity" is coined from the Latin word—Identitat, which means "Same and same." It implies, "probably from." It is a word used in tracing the origin or evolution of most things in the tale of existence.

Everything on the surface of the Earth has an identity; be it the blue-green algae, hydra, ferns, and even we humans are known as the Homo sapiens.

Daily, we keep learning, striving, and meeting additional people. At the instance of the phrase "meeting", pleasantries becomes a likely occurrence that realistically births the word—identity. But Bro Steve, how do you mean? Yeah, the fact is this; at the initial state of every recent conversation, identities are being exchanged between two or more group of people; species, races, tribes, etc.

We live in a time when the only thing that speaks for us aside from the Celestial participation is our identity. The world today is turning out to be a discrepancy between its flora and fauna; effecting a lot of occurrences in the tale of existence.

Citing its effect on humans, it has affected the entire human race, physically, emotionally, and psychologically.

Come with me to my country-Nigeria, this is a nation where the term "Identity", is recognised and held in awe among her citizens. Usually, there is this common question asked among the unlucky folks; mostly amongst the unemployed fellows who can't meet up with the responsibility of putting up with care. The question goes like this; You get connection? I know it sounds like a phrase, but it a question asked with the aid of the Nigeria Pidgin-English. What does it mean? It is so simple! What it means is this; "if you don't have an identity wherever you going to run an errand, you will nothing but stumble."

Unfortunately, it was never so in the early 90s, and even the era preceding. But as civilization progresses, everything grows in terms of magnitude, relevance, etc. The difference in operation is clear between the last three-decade and our present time. So, as time passes by, negative intuitions evolved from one form to form causing more problems for the present era and to the unborn generation.

Women of honour are entities whose identity cannot be disregarded anywhere in the entire universe. It is true not just today but right from the generation as of old till date. The identity of every woman or lady is the inscription of what she truly portrays. It might be good deeds, poor reputation, shy temperament, aggressive and meekly behavioural caption, beautiful not ugly purposes, etc. What counts is your Identify!

Never forget, you are on earth for the basis of representing a tribe in the city of Zion. You can't afford to dishearten them by subscribing to an awful identity.

SPLENDOUR

"Ladies and women of honour are the radiators of God's glory." — Stephen Edoh.

Splendour is a word that reveals the impressive beauty of something; it could be a being, an object, or the rhetorical things of nature. The splendour of every lady and woman of honour is her light that shines so brightly in the deadliest phases of life. Her aura linked to a compartment that brings forth the delightful fragrances of nature. On her face denotes a smile that deciphered from the throne room in Zion.

God is so huge for a single man to tell of His glory. He shows his glorious splendour in the life of men and women, ladies and gentlemen, boys and girls, etc. What am I trying to convey? The seed of God is in everyone, but then, only those that realised so blossoms. Our character identity must denote the doing, and dealings of God, irrespective of the difference in background, and civilization.

The tale of beauty emerged via Potters skill in dealing with clay. God is the potter, while you are the clay in reference. When God created you in your Momma's womb, He did something startling; erecting a vessel in His reputation and likeness. Wow, it's amazing! Do you know why? The reason is this; You look like God and your beauty represents His glorious splendour.

The Supreme God created no one to show a mystery or dimension of a unique kind, other than that which brings glory to His name. At most times, you marvelled to because of your beauty, level of intelligence, striking voice, etc. But then you recall that God made you so fulfil His wishes on Earth. If, at any point, you give glory to your parent for your beauty, then you trigger the jealousy of God.

Our gifts and talents are the display of God's glorious grandeur here on Earth. The uniqueness, beauty, excellency, and usefulness of our various gifts out there denote the few among the many spectacular features found in God. Never forget, your gifts are profitable to you, your family and the entire denizens of the Earth. But it's an instrument used in honouring God. From now on, use that voice, talent, to honour God.

The riches and wealth of this world all arose from his approval. Biblically, it was in scripted that, "He Giveth power to get wealth." What a God we serve! Today many people out there is living a luxurious lifestyle, neglecting their maker and to the poor. But thatch remains the same; they will one day die, leave, and be brought to the throne judgement. Note this; any riches or wealth that doesn't aid the work of God's kingdom translates on the track lane of vanity.

Today, most women are victims of all the points I've laid out in the series. Unfortunately, it deters them from becoming a cause of celebration in the sight of men. Every woman of honour gives birth to a true identity that speaks for her, and splendour is a vital part of the prerequisites that triggers honour.

Identity results from glorious splendour. In the series of life, we have to value, cherish, and appreciate the dealings of God in our lives. Unfortunately, with many, it differs. It's not exemplary for anyone administers beneath the glory of God to ignore the fact of bestowing thanks to the Celestial King. Thanksgiving is one dialect in Zion that God understands.

Therefore, let our beauty, gifts, riches, all be for bringing glory to God.

TRUSTWORTHINESS

"Ladies and Women whose attitudes are traceable to trustworthiness are entities of honour." – Stephen Edoh.

The word ''trustworthiness'' means a lot; reliability, dependability, steadfastness, etc. It's a virtue that conveys trust, love, confidence, hope, reliance, and many more! It is the foundation that lays the block of a long-term friendship, relationship, or perhaps a team success.

Trustworthiness is the bedrock of every friendship, relationship on which success becomes an actuality. It is the character of virtue of every woman or lady of honour. In its absence, it becomes a problem for many people to shift level in relationships and marriages. Unfortunately, it's linked to a rare commodity, not that common; only a few persons process this feature.

They are a lot of women, but when you attempt to further categorise them, you will find out they are another set of women known as, "the women of honour". That's the difference!

Women of honour are entities that are accelerated by a worthy state of trust. It's a thing of pride and joy, when you are viewed or seen as a trustworthy fellow. It's fascinating! The benefits disseminated by this character virtue defines a moderate, a terrific occurrence. Not just that; it breaks the law of magnetism; it attracts humans of diverse temperaments and personalities.

We cannot overemphasise the tangibility of a lifestyle detail by trustworthiness because of its countless windfalls enjoyed by the subscribers of its character virtue. Shortly, we shall gear up for a pleasant tale all about trustworthiness that took effect in the animal kingdom. Before then, I've to bring this to your awareness: no negative temperament can't outclass trust because it is a factor of truthfulness that sets the masses free.

Once upon a time in the animal kingdom, there lives a billy goat called, "Ewu" and a lion named, "Agaba." Too, there was a tortoise named, "Epee" and the other animals with their various names., Agaba the lion while chasing after a prey got caught by a trap; somewhat like a prison cell. Fortunately, Ewu the billy goat was strolling down the hill to search out goodies for his four chambers, when he surprises found Agaba looking sad in the dungeon. On noticing Ewu, his Agaba was saturated by an aura of joy.

Without hesitating, he pleaded for aid to effect his liberation. But then, Ewu bade that he must sign a memorandum of trustworthiness, of which Agaba hurriedly did as proposed. Soon after, the story becomes a prevaricated tale; Agaba grabbed Ewu by the neck, preparing to devour him after days of staying hungry. But then Ewu reminds Agaba of the memo he signed. Still, it turns out to be a quarrel between the duals.

But here come Epee, the Tortoise and the companies of other animals.

Upon hearing their argument, all the animals excluding Epe backed Agaba because of fear. Epee pretending not to comprehend the entire issue asked Agaba of the place Ewu found him. He pointed at the spot, Epe then asked him to show them how he sat upon Ewu, He did hurriedly. But then Epe shut down the door!

Guess what? The whole animals were shocked. They asked, Epee why? This was his response, "if we let him eat Ewu today, some other day he will fall hungry, and one of us will be devoured." Darling, what have you learnt from this story? A lot, I guessed. Yeah, it a tale of trustworthiness. Just think of this; if only the lion has inclined to his promise by acting trustworthy, he wouldn't have gone back to the dungeon. Unfortunately, he went back and perished.

In the series of life, you are likely to come across many Agaba's, but then you don't have to act like those fearful animals because nemesis hit the camp of the untruthful and unfaithful fellows. If only you will be a trustworthy individual, you and your household will eat the best of fruits and the drink of the sweetest honey till Hades calls. Betrayal is the act and doings of the mundane woman, Trust is the character virtue of an honourable woman.

Never forget the law of honest demands, total submission to its other laws. You might ask, but why? Here is the answer to your question, "Every good advice is profitable for the body, also its triggers the act of giving thanks and rendering appreciation to God." Learning to live a life that denotes trustworthiness Is the same as learning to value, appreciate, and cherish the people in your life. Not just the people in your life, but to the God we served.

Stay with me.

INTERCESSORY

"One reason the Biblical day's apostle, Paul could do greater works than his companions took a conclusion from the help of intercessors." – Stephen Edoh.

Who is an intercessor? One, who God has made a spiritual custodian over a territory; legislating and coding on the behalf of the territory in the spirit realm. Intercessors are the emitters of lights in every given territory or axis. They don't just code and legislate; decision and commanding power live in them. Samuel was one. Deborah was another. Too, John Wesley, Kathryn Kuhlman, Maria Etter—Woodworth, and the Generals of old were part of the team. These are custodians and territorial commanders!

In a time when the whirlwind and forces of Hades are contending against the children and the church of God, intercessors act as the liberating general between the children of God and the powerful forces of Hell. Until intercessors arise, a territory still maintains a state of static motion in her given affairs and dealings. The power of intercession is stronger than the influence of money.

Today, many people still intercede for their territory, but at this moment we will cite our focus on the state of every family; praying for family members and friends besides. Too, we shall discuss the facts and benefits of interceding for our given territories. We gat something spectacular to explore. It will be a pleasant adventure. I just request you stay calm and enjoy the series ahead.

I cite the strength of every home foundation on the prayers of the manager:[wife or mother] of that house. In every progressive home, success is only a story because in it lives a woman who codes and legislate the governance of that home in the realm of the deep. Ladies and woman who intercede, code, and legislate are missiles fired from the horizon of Zion. Mighty women such as Kathryn Kuhlman, Maria Woodworth-Etter were not just prayer warriors or intercessors. They were invaders of regions: reigning and taking charge of territorial dominion.

The first step in building a violent free home is by establishing the relationship or marriage on the platform of prayers. This is because anything that operates outside the aura of prayer functioned in the state of bewilderment. Most relationships have failed today because they have shut the prayer room of that relationship down. Someone might ask, but how can a prayer room be shut down? Pleasant question! Here is the answer, "Whenever misunderstanding take hold of a relationship and it's not addressed as fast as possible, the spirit of prayer leave till the room becomes empty and void."

When you encounter an aligned woman, in a moment you discover a successful home manager, whose influences triggers the formation of a godly citadel, and the upbringing of virtuous children. The hegemony of prayer outclassed the influence of wealth. Women and ladies that pray are the ones that bear fruits and produce undeniable results in the series of life. You don't dream to have a better home, no! You pray and travail to have a promising home.

Praying for your family and friends is a display of a character virtue that entice the blessings of God to your life. When we pray for our family, it's not only headlining the proof of care but also of love. Women of honour are vessels of prayers. Deborah prays. Mother Teresa prays. Too, generals such as Kathryn Kuhlman, Maria Etter—Woodworth, Pandita

Ramabai, Anna, Priscilla and many others pray. Evil plots planned and effected from the directorate of hell against godly families get annihilated only on the altar of prayers.

Friends are the instrument for changes that translate to transform our lives either for good or evil. However, it's vital and essential that you find time praying for your friends; for this reason, you are acknowledged as a woman of honour. The success story of every relationship or friendship becomes effective on the altar of prayer and supplication. Prayer is the pathway on which we flourish as we maintain continuous motion communication with our Celestial father.

The Wesley brothers and George Whitefield maintained a continuous dispute free friendship up to the very moment they left to join the other patriarchs in Zion. But all this took effect because they positioned their friendship and brotherhood on the altar of prayer. Until our relationship and friendships work and function according to the dealings and transactions of the prayer room. We stride to the hallway of intricacy. When you learn to pray for friends and relatives, God enjoys His intimacy with you.

Our territories are the axis where our territorial dominion becomes effective for clarifying and translating the rhythm of Zion to the denizens of the Earth. The decisive power of God wouldn't be effective in the mortal's realm without the consent of man. He wouldn't come and turn around the captivity of territory in the absence of willing and aligned men. This is the reason men such as John Wesley could walk across a region, and transformation takes effect; all because he was aligned and a man of prayer.

When you come to a full conclusion of becoming a spiritual watchdog over your territory, you embark on the journey of paving way for the progress and growth of your territory. The strength of intercession is more potent than the prestige of wealth as I earlier said. Nations such as the United States, United Kingdom, China, with Russia, Korea, Germany,., are dominating the world today in various sectors only because great patriarchs of old form these regions coded and legislated the success of these lands in the time past.

Today, many people's thoughts that the poor state of several territories took effect from the existence of poor leadership. Yeah, they are partially right. But the factual justification of this fiasco results from the absence of intercessors. Women are too part of this great revival that was awakened many years ago. Darling, be part of it. You must stand up and intercede for your territory, state, or country. It might seem weird to you, but it isn't!

It's time you become an intercessor, if perhaps you aren't one. The light of your territory might be abode in you being the forerunner. Never forget this, "Intercessors are beacons of light." Don't slay away this outstanding privilege by skipping the chance of becoming an intercessor. It pays!

Stay with me.

We believe that this very chapter has blessed you. It will be an honour to be of good counsel to you. More so, it would be more pleasurable to receive help from you.

Stephen Edoh Ministries and Words Citadel Family needs your partner-ship to continue to spread God's words via writing to the nations.

We need your support. It could be monthly remittance, perhaps just a moment's help.

Further, we are available to help you with good counsel, and words of Hope that will brings about restoration in all aspects of life.

Remember, that we are your friends and you can reach out to us with the email below.

Indeed, there is no price tag for every counsel offered. It is free of charge.

You can send your partnership or one-time support payment through our PayPal email address below.

You can also testify to how this book has impacted your life using the same email below.

We love and care for you.

PayPal payment email address: **Stephenedoh2000@gmail.com**

Pay Pal link: **www.Paypal.me/StephenEdoh**

Thank you and many blessings to you and your family.

Preference

"Our choices are the very indicator of our life stories."—Stephen Edoh.

I precisely understand "preference" to be choices, intentions, opinionns, in the various multi-lingual dialects around the entire universe. It is the reference point to which emerged every decision in the series of life. Life without preference isn't an actuality; because in the series of life, choices lead and prevails. Just imagine being brought forth into the world and you are choosing less, then you seem to be a living dead.

The first humans on Earth, "Adam and Eve" made it a choice to defile the rule that God imposed in the imperial terrace of Eden, but guesses what happened, they got sacked and was sent packing from the grand garden. Nothing works and prevails without a choice or choices on the Earth crust. Why? The reason is this; choices are the compact that drives, direct, and pivot our life; either to the threshold of negativism or positionvism.

In the series of life, you are led by a thought translating for good or that exemplifying evil. The preference of every man and woman on the Earth surface must connote an expression of the good deeds that detail positivism and equipped men for multidimensional impact. When the intentions, views, and choices of a man aren't in alignment with thoughts of good, the occurrences of evil translate into reality.

God defines a state of love the very moment He chose not to coerce Adam to do His will, other than give to him sets of instruction to obey. Unfortunately, Adam and his wife, Eve, declined God with their act of subscription to the wrong preference. We become preys of nemesis, the very moment we subscribed to sin. The neverse is the case when talking about those with cordial, spirited, and sound led preference.

The character identity of every woman of honour distinguished not in her culture, but in her capacity to discern the things suitable for her. It is noteworthy to conceal of the fact that, "Every woman of honour is an accurate definition or portrayal of a precise and genuine led intention."

At a certain stage in the tale of existence, there arose a time when the whirlwind of coercion arm-twist the decision phase of several individuals on the top surface of the Earth crust. Such wind could be in the form of bribery, nepotism, embezzlement, and other forms of corrupt practices.

However, the joyful news is this, within that period, only those with a positive difference and status of honorarium posture firmly.

Ene prefers gowns, Ehi love suit, while Ihotu enjoys wearing native blouses. Do you comprehend? These ladies all have their wears of preference. That you are a lady with a positive difference is a sign that you are likely to battle with the emphasis of preference. Ladies and women of honour learn to make positive choices because the effect of choice in a moment could better nor destroys the life of an individual forever.

Choices and preference are synonymous with workplace ethics. The tangible nature of workplace ethics is so strict for anyone to bypass. It too applies to preference; making the wrong choice destroys the excellent reputation of an individual either for a moment or beyond.

Never, pick to the wrong choice of anyone, let your yes standstill, the same goes with your no. Your friends and antagonist might view you to be a mundane kind, detail your dressing as old-fashioned, ascribed to your hairstyle as locally weaved, etc. But the tangibility of womanhood and the status of honorarium stands firm. Darling, their tale is a caption of a parrot cry. Giving heels to such a tale end one in a cycle of mess.

Adherence to the right voice in the series of life isn't a resultant effect of good deeds, but a translation that influences the doings and actions from the frontiers of Zion. Ladies and women of honour are a set of excellent translators of the Zionist tongue; a dialect understood and spoken by entities in the beautiful city of Zion. Until the right choice is made, the blessings meant for an individual stays a step away.

In these last days, God is searching for men and women who will translate the rhythm of the end-time revival to the denizens of the Earth, and to bring men into the light of Jesus. The pleasant news I have for you is this; Jesus has chosen you as one missionary from the frontiers of Zion that will take the revival fire down to the end of the Earth. It's never something you have to think twice about. The time is now. Be a revivalist.

THE BRIDE OF JESUS

"Jesus bought your nody for a cost that can't be estimated in earthly currency." —Stephen Edoh.

Who is the bride of Jesus? The doers of his word and those whose life emit light. Every woman of honour is a godly woman, and every godly woman is a bride of the glorious King, Jesus. What such of undeserving privilege and honour is it to be called, "The Bride Of Jesus,". Unfortunately, many people missed their chance of being called, "Bride of Jesus" because of the odd display in their character.

The bride of the Glorious king is one whose personality and temperament display the splendour and the glorious grandeur of Jesus. She is the daughter of the highest king, an oracle of love, a platter of ideas, the Lily of the Valley, and a lover of the poor. None can define her to be a harsh or fierce type; because she's an oracle of love. Her lifestyle cann't be linked to the secular world; because she's a delightful princess from the city of Zion.

Peace is one attribute to be constituted when conversing about the bride of Jesus. Her life isn't a tale and inscription of a battlefield. No! She's a citadel of peace and serenity. In her camp, one finds consolation and comfort. King Solomon in his song of songs tale refers to her as his beloved. She carries the DNA of unity and wholeness in her chromosome. When trying to describe who she truly is, you refer to her this way, "the nucleus of stability."

She's called the bride of Jesus not because of her beauty, charisma or splendour, but because of her sound led preference. Her life never translates on the things on civilization and secularism. She's a woman of godly intents and connotations. Never will you find her making decisions that aim for her good alone. No! She's not the voracious or selfish

41

type, but one who mastermind success for her household and the entire universe. What a distinguished bride she is!

THE RED HOT REVIVAL

"Gone are the days of Kathryn Kuhlman and Maria Etter-Woodward, when women understood the dynamics and vigorousness of the end-time revival," — Stephen Edoh.

The major goal of, or reason for, the end-time revival is to first bring men to the phase of repentance and then into the light of Jesus. Revival is as old as a man. Starting from the days of John the Baptist; who went on baptising men down to the time of our own experience. The biblical disciples of Jesus turned Apostles were the first in taking the red hot revival down to the horizon of the Earth. Later, men such as John Wycliffe, William Tyndale, John Wesley, George Whitefield, William Branham, Charles Wesley, and the General's of old, joined the wagon in heralding the red hot revival.

Revival is a language of the ancient paths. Only custodians and Generals of old could decode and encode in this language. Great, patriarch such as John Wesley travelled miles upon miles teaching the word of God, performing miracles, and bringing men into the light of Jesus. They were none as John Wesley, who travelled such a range from one horizon of the Earth to another, translating the rhythm of the red hot revival in his days.

The effect of the red hot revival didn't just translate in words alone but tunes and sounds. Charles Wesley, the biological and spiritual brother of

John Wesley, was one of those who translated the effects of the red hot revival via tunes from frontiers of Zion. He was not just a chorister; he was a vocalist and a revivalist from the city of Zion; a house of innumerable angels and Saints, the dwelling place of the Celestial bodies.

However, the story didn't stop there. Another feminist from Zion arrived in the person of Maria Woodworth-Etter. Having given her life to Jesus Christ at thirteen, she heard the call of God. Of her calling, she would later write, "I heard the voice of Jesus calling me to go out in the highway and hedges and gather the lost sheep." Unfortunately, Maria faced pains and travails in her lifetime; from divorcing her first husband to marrying the second one, of which she lost 5 of his six kids to Hades.

In 1902, she married a man named Samuel Etter, who later died in 1914. Afterwards, the search and studying of Scriptures become a daily routine. Come next, was the preaching of the Lord's divine healing. It didn't take long to observe that evangelism and healing went hand in hand as thousands of souls were won to Christ because of seeing others healed. To cut the lengthy story short, Sister Maria–Etter pioneered the way tor Pentecostal manifestations that are so common in the Charismatic and Pentecostal bodies today.

The above nobles mentioned in this series only fulfilled their purpose, because they made the right choice. Their intents were clear, no stain was found on their destiny regalia. The truth remains the same, none ever fulfil the demands of their destiny in the omission of sound preference. Jesus made it a choice to reject the plea of the devil because He knew an accolade await Him in the city of Zion. In the end, the son of man was glorified.

Dating

"**E**very marital thought initiated by God stirs up a relationship that ends in the state of delight,"—Stephen Edoh.

Dating is a stage where an individual enters a relationship to feel loved, get married, and to fulfil his or her purpose. Every relationship takes effect for one reason or the other, but purity leads the God-approved kind of relationship. It's in dating an individual come to find their match in every aspect; Character, culture, etc.

God is our father, maker, and of all, our one and true king. When God made man, He found out himself that man needed helpmeet to fulfil the tasks He assigned to the man in the garden of Eden. Then He gave him a woman. The first man and woman to live on the Earth surface are no new individuals to our awareness other than the dual combination of Adam and Eve.

In the tale of existence, God has a plan for everyone to get married, multiply, and also bring glory to His holy name. But then marriage doesn't just take effect without going through a process or several processes. It has to glide through several phases before it becomes an actuality. It is a must for you to know what dating is more concerned about; It views, goals, and positive impact in the life of a virtuous lady, or woman. The success behind every marriage is first uncovered during dating. Most times people decide due to the absence of a substitute for a certain commodity. The same goes with humans; tying the knot with someone because she was the only individual willing and available. Unfortunately, they end up with the wrong person.

As a lady on the verge of entering a relationship, recall that only a stable mind-set flirts with a good and delightful aura. If you aren't cautious in saying yes to the wrong person, then you are liable to start a fictitious life that will wander in the cycle of complexity, except the hands of God intervene.

Most ladies today in no hesitation say yes to the seeker of the aroma because of a discrepancy in life; poverty, unemployment, unhappiness, etc. But it isn't a prudent move taken by many ladies; accepting relationship proposals hastily, all because of frustration. Unfortunately, it all results from thoughtlessness. The fact remains the same; Ladies and a woman of honour don't dance to the melody of plight. It's a prime time we explore more on dating and know further of its consequence and how to succeed through the phase of the singleton. I do believe you have a lot to learn in the countless of series you are likely to come across in this journey to your prime.

WHY DATING?

"In every titration reaction there is always an endpoint, and in bother, for you to determine the endpoint and it there values; Use an indicator," — Stephen Edoh.

When you reason through the question, "Why dating?", you will agree with me on the fact that a majority of people in this advanced era doesn't have a better answer to the above-asked question. With some, it differs; maybe dating for ungodly pleasures; sex, kiss, romance, etc. However, the concept of dating is beyond such comprehension. The art and science of glimpsing dating as a dimension that pioneers several mundane occurrences birthed from nothing but ignorance.

Thoughtlessness is the architect of ignorance, and this is the reason men fail, struggle and end up leaving the Earth realm without translating their purpose from the track lane of Zion. As a lady of honour, your goal is not to have the godliest, handsome, rich, famous, or captivating guy. But to pioneers these features; godliness, handsomeness, riches, fame, etc., into him.

Stay with me, please, as we sail further.

READINESS

"Until a woman prepares her heart for a task, she cannot fulfil the goal of the task assigned to her." —Stephen Edoh.

Readiness is the foundation or building block of every success story. It is the nucleus of every positive decision that begat victories. Every victorious team in history were initiated into an aura of conquest and triumph by the impact of readiness. In the absence of readiness, failure becomes the leading news in the affairs of life.

Readiness isn't an illustration that results from the vibes of one's desperation for success. But that which emerged from the consciousness of a purpose. It standstill because we learn to succeed better in the series of life endeavours when we act in readiness. How I do mean darling? At the instance of every brilliant move, readiness plays an essential and incredible role that engineers success into reality.

At a point in life when a lady isn't ready to go into a relationship, her status of intimacy inscribed a state of rest or static motion. The vision of every lady is to have happiness and do exploits in marriage, but the sure fact here is this; it all translate from the instincts of readiness. Every ready heart is the centre focal point of victory. Until you leave the state of rest, your craving to be in motion appears void!

The tangibility of readiness cannot be overemphasised because its effects rely on the encoder of these blissful words conveyed here to exclusively decode it into his or her life. You need to be too conscious of something significant; when you're not prepared for a relationship, stay single, else, you suffer heartbreak and traumas. In the series of life, it is no news that success in marriage results from the wife readiness once as a spinster-to say, "Yes we can."

We have soared this far, and I surely believed you have learned so much in this series. I want to ask you this question if perhaps you aren't dating, are you ready to date? A quest meant for you alone.

MARRIAGE

"Every success story that took effect without the backing of a woman or a lady is a tedious tale,, —Stephen Edoh

Marriage is a rite that initiates a man and a woman into a physical and spiritual union for them both to become couples; husband and wife. It is also the act of wiping out the singleton chronology to putting down a nuptial anecdote. We live in a time, when most ladies dance to the whirlwind of civilization, rather than driving back to Jesus. Unfortunately, they adore a style of life detailed by the complexness, concluding on the fact that the devil got them into a state of constraint.

One challenge faced these days in several countless marriages around the world result from an awful structure of the decision put up with; either by the wife of a man or the husband of a woman. The ability of a marriage to fulfil its blissful destinies rely on the decision a lady take as a spinster. Until you realise that dating is the first dimension to lay down the blocks of a successful marriage, you will not propel your dream home into a delightful emotion.

Marriage is not just a reason for one to enter a relationship. It is an occurrence translated in the life of a man by God from the city of Zion, for the sake of multiplication of humans in large digits and in a clear reverence, worship Him. Most times, when people go into a relationship, one can fully concord to the fact that yes, they want to get married.

Dating is not just a platform that brings two sets of people into marriage. It's a school in the realm of love, where bachelors and spinsters learn the moves, and the do and undo in marriage. It is a platform where you come to understand the character, culture, and challenges faced by your soon to be spouse. Don't forget, if an individual cannot meet up with the fact of discerning the culture of his or her partner, divorce becomes a possible occurrence.

Recall that dating isn't just a platform that initiates marriage, but that which has the capacity in its cradle phase to decide the fate of a marriage. Besides, marriage isn't just an experience that transpired from dating but appears to be one of the essential reasons people go into a relationship.

PURPOSE

"At a certain stage in life, everyone to need have an intimate friend in other to soar to the hilltop of life," —Stephen Edoh.

Purpose is a goal or aim bestowed on an individual, in other, for a translation to take effect from the Frontiers of Zion. It is the exclusion of man's will and the inclusion of God's will. It is the difference between our calling and earthly desires. Our calling is being espoused by the very purpose we are here on earth to fulfil. While our earthly desires are pioneered by hard work, persistence, determination, and passion.

In a time and season when the whirlwind of life blows so hard on the earth surface, it takes only purpose for a woman of honour to know her stand. The life of every woman of purpose is an interesting poem being read by trailblazers and mighty subjugators of age. What makes a lady, a woman of honour, is a purpose. As a lady with a positive difference, your beauty and character aren't all you need to legs it into the hall of fame. What certified you as a woman of honour is the realisation of purpose.

Every relationship must be purpose-driven, else, it suffers a state of trauma detailed by mediocrity and indifference. In the omission of the word, "purpose" in a relationship, the dual partners strides on the hallway of uproar and discomforts. This is the reason most home ends up struggling to survive collisions that provoked unrest and anxieties. When the purpose is discovered in a relationship, it walks down, not just to marriage but to history. One of the beautiful decision you could ever put up with is to discover purpose before excluding the singleton chronology to starting the nuptial anecdote.

Dating is a platform that creates an atmosphere for uncovering several things in the tale of life. Unfortunately, the most relationship suffers from distress and setbacks due to a style of life known as parasitism. Jesus made a stunning statement in his days, "Many will come in my name,". This same statement translates in many relationships; a guy could conclude that he loves a lady, unfortunately, he's only sucking the sweet part of her nectar; deluding her to believe his fictitious actions. As a lady with a difference, be sound and spiritual in discerning the right man meant for you, else, the ravenous wolf in his polished regalia end up devouring you.

Purpose must displace the trace of greed and selfishness in a relationship. Every love association that operates under the influence of covetousness and greediness doesn't take a bit of advanced step, rather it downshifts day after day, seconds after seconds. Your life isn't a portal for another person success when you act as a former and not as a reformer.

We believe that this very chapter has blessed you. It will be an honour to be of good counsel to you. More so, it would be more pleasurable to receive help from you.

Stephen Edoh Ministries and Words Citadel Family needs your partnership to continue to spread God's words via writing to the nations.

We need your support. It could be monthly remittance, perhaps just a moment's help.

Further, we are available to help you with good counsel, and words of Hope that will brings about restoration in all aspects of life.

Remember, that we are your friends and you can reach out to us with the email below.

Indeed, there is no price tag for every counsel offered. It is free of charge.

You can send your partnership or one-time support payment through our PayPal email address below.

You can also testify to how this book has impacted your life using the same email below.

We love and care for you.

PayPal payment email address: **Stephenedoh2000@gmail.com**

Pay Pal link: **www.Paypal.me/StephenEdoh**

Thank you and many blessings to you and your family.

Purity

"Until a civilization embraces a lifestyle that is gleamed by purity, God's glory will be distant from them." —Stephen Edoh.

The phrase "purity" is coined from two separate words in the Latin lingo; "Purus" which mean pure, and "Puritat" which implies the absence of evil impressions or guilt. Furthermore, it cites a lifestyle that transpired from the influence of holiness, decency, and motive distinguished by positivism. Indeed, purity is the translation of the God kind of lifestyle into reality.

Walking in purity is a clear connotation of walking in light.

As most times, when the denizens of a certain region relinquish the whirlwind of civilization, and subsequently, submit to the influence of purity, God appeared to them in His glorious influence and then they flourish. The effect of purity is the tale of greatness and blessings initiated by the celestial sovereignty

Purity is a culture that impact the nature of Jesus into the life of a typical or mundane man. It's not just a sort of styles that detail goodness, it is goodness itself. Every woman, lady, or girl child yearning to become a woman must be coordinated and influenced by thoughts details by piousness, kind heartedness, and peace.

TEAM PURITY

"Only a team that walk in purity flourishes. In exception, such a team strides on the hallway of civilization,"- Stephen Edoh.

Purity is a culture as I earlier said, it isn't a fact of intuition but an actuality glimpsed in the life of people. It effects result to the conclusion of what we understood to be a team. Additionally, the translation of purity in a team rely on the willingness of the team to adopt it as an ordinance.

Every team has a culture, formula, strategy, and blueprint. So, the same with you a lifestyle detail by purity. You are not like those mundane lady out there, no! You are a woman of honour, you have a blueprint and you belong to a mighty and fierce team.

A woman of honour is a woman of spiritual sportsmanship. She's the star player in the team purity. What a notable captain she is! The commander and pioneer of her team success. She's not a looser but a winner. Failure and defeat isn't an option for her because she flourish as an envoy of God's present.

When the whirlwind of secularism and corruption blow in her direction, she stand firm. Her physique is distinguished as compared to the army of locust as detailed by the biblical Prophet—Joel in his " Army of Locust " vision. Every woman, lady, and girl child that belongs to the team purity, is a principal factor in most of the success stories in the tale of existence.

When a woman or a lady or a girl child lives and function outside ordinances of the team purity, she's no longer of God but of all the world. Purity edify not just the body of a woman but her souls. God is well pleased when the life of any woman is led by purity.

Purity is not just a criterion for becoming or a criteria to become a woman of honour. It's the most fundamental organ of a virtuous woman. When the heart taken off the body of a man, he vanish away to the portal of Hades. The same goes for a woman of honour; as soon as purity becomes absent in her life, she then dance to the whirlwind of sin.

It's not an advice or an opinion if you are being told to remain purity-led, it actually a secret revealed for free. Stay with me, the journey of a great start with a few steps that later translate into a wishes.

THE HOLY SPIRIT

" Only the Holy Spirit can oversee our life to effectively function in the dimensions of God's module operandi, " —Stephen Edoh.

Purity is one of the dimensions of God module operandi and only the Holy Spirit can aid us in living a life that translate on the lane of righteousness. It's the character identity of the Holy Spirit; His virtue, personality, charisma, jovialness, etc. In the time past, before the Era of Jesus, it's was difficult to access, clarify, and put down the dealings of God, except for the Prophets and priests in those days. But in the series, we shall be exploring a bit of the life and impact of the Holy Spirit.

The Holy Spirit is the divine influencer that impacts the instincts of heroism and bravery into the bloodstream of men who are willing and cleaned off sin. He is the spirit entity that triggers the hormones of a typical man with courage and determination to exclude the advent of fear in the trials of life. Today, a lot of so-called Christians suffers from insecurity and symptoms of phobia due to the absence of the Holy Spirit.

The Bible reminds of the fact that He hasn't given us the spirit, nature, and aura of fear but of sound mind. Wow, our God is so amazing! Think of it darling, "not of fear, but of sound mind." If only a lot of people out there will comprehend the statement above as a promise and not mere words, then fear and insecurity will be conquered.

Women of honour are the adventurous and audacious set of entities whose personalities cannot be shuffled to the ground level, by fear nor vulnerability. They are vessels of the divine spirit; that's why the essence of bravery and confidence findeth expression in their life. Thus, only the Holy Spirit giveth bravery and liberation.

Fear is one reason why men fail to fulfil a purpose.

When the Holy Spirit becomes the central focal point of every vision and dream, purpose strides to suit a realistic experience translated from the horizons of Zion. The divine spirit of God is the only pioneer that aid men in fulfilling their heavenly mandate here on Earth. We become part of the set of entities that travail under the influence of mediocrity and indifference when the Holy Spirit lives outta the borders of our life.

Negligence to adhering to the tune of the Holy Spirit is a reason why a lot of men have ceased to function in their places of calling today.

Intil men arise and align with the frequency of the Holy Spirit, they will continue to keep the hyoue in the state of intricacy. Today, they are a lot of dudes replenished with a lot of talents and possibilities in our society. Unfortunately, the portals to which the unveiling of their beautiful talents take verdict sealed up due to the deprivation of the holy spirit. When a generation agrees to transact and stream with the Holy Spirit, their land flow with milk and honey. But in a state when the denizens of the Earth neglect the divine spirit, such generation strides to the coliseum of misery.

He is the spirit of excellence and uniqueness, pioneer of success and victory, the giver of wisdom and understanding, etc. In a time when the hamlet of Zion calls for the denizens of the earth to align and fulfil the purpose of the great monarch, only the Holy Spirit helps to translate that intuition. He alone giveth gifts to men, knowledge to problem-solver, etc. Men need the holy spirit to grow.

No woman ever fulfil the dream of building a godly citadel in the absence of excellence and wisdom. The Holy Spirit aid every woman of honour in raising godly youngsters and kids that shows up to become vessels that will herald the revival to the perimeter of the earth. Too, the advancement of every home resides in the knowledge of the holy ghost. But the fact remains the same, only the Holy Spirit aids all these into reality.

The Holy Spirit is the spirit that gives rise to peace in every godly home. In him alone we find serenity and solace, joy and happiness, honour and resplendence. Our Lord Jesus Christ reminds the disciples of the coming of the comforting spirit; one and will give to the rest and relaxation, consolation and mitigation for the effective functioning of the Spirit man. And after the delightful Messiah has ascended to the Celestial Realm, the divine spirit appeared as promised. It's a high time you invite Him to your home for a total turnaround to take effect.

Finally, the Holy Spirit is the pioneer of Holiness in the life of believers. David the biblical custodian once said, " Cast not your Holy Spirit away from my present. " I love the statement David made. Truly, the Holy Spirit is so precious for us to ignore, neglect, or avoid. When He is with us, sins and transgressions flew from our life. Afterwards, We become alabaster in His hands used in erecting a beautiful and magnificent vessel that brings glory to God.

Holiness is the character virtue for every lady or woman to cultivate and aid their journey to the hallway of honour. The Holy Spirit is glad and happy each time we live and work in purity. Nothing excites him than the feelings of the glory and honour that await us in the end. You need the Holy Spirit ever than you think you need him. At all times, you have to bring everything in obedience to Christ, but then only a life that wanders in the cycle of holiness can effect such a proposal.

When a woman or a lady live and submit her home on the triggering platform of the holy spirit, she enters into transactions that change she and her household from the Men of the street to entities who are kingdom Remnant. There is no life out the life of holiness because Holiness is the way, and too, it is life. None can do without it except such as looking forward to seeing the place of solace in Hades. Holiness is life because it is found life.

Stay with me!

Melancholy

"It takes a lot of struggles to find joy in this tragic world. Only Jesus can oversee us into the hallway of ecstasy," — Stephen Edoh.

Melancholy is a state or condition blurred by sentiment initiated via several negative occurrences such as sorrow, grief, anxiety, disappointment. It's a syndrome in the serenity phase of an individual life, or perhaps a group of people. Too, it is the difference between the two crucial moments; Happiness and Unhappiness in the time and seasons of life.

Every life carrier organism faces a reality of struggle and pain at a certain time in the series of life. Jesus never told us that the storm wouldn't surface, but he let us infer that smooth sailing is guaranteed. In the series of life, every struggle and challenge is a therapy that triggers our hormones to prepare for the days of glory. In the absence of a struggle, there isn't a tale of victory to theorise.

Life is about living to learn, also learning to fulfil a purpose. Unfortunately, at a certain period in life, we experience several negative occurrences. Sometimes, it is not our desire to witness the odd stuff of nature that's taking effect in our lives; that of ours and our entire family.

But joyful and blissful moments accompanied the travails witnessed in every true and positive espoused life story.

In the series of life, there isn't a secret to living a life that excludes pains and turbulent moments. Even as a Christian, there is a certain period the devil subscribes to causing us pain, but we just have to watch and pray, also keep a strong stand in our most holy place. The series of difficulties we encounter daily come to a timely end at a certain moment we realised our worth and value, and our authority in Christ.

As a lady with differences, it has to jingle through your genius cavity — [the brain] of the fact that, "every arduous moment you encountered is a stepping stone on your journey to womanhood."

Often, the odd moments we confront in life strive to mimic the travail of a woman in labour. At a stage, when things seem not to be working, many people become more confused, finding it hard to know their way out. Most times, they even contemplate on giving up, leading to the birth of several negative occurrences amongst others such as suicide, drunkenness, prostitution. But you know what? Giving up isn't the way out.

We live in a time when the flora and fauna of an evergreen world are trembling. A lot of unrest and confusions are taking charge of the dimensions and domains of authority and jurisdictions. In a time when many people travails in the misery mood to carter for their beloved family. But these don't translate to the fact we have to give up, instead, it calls for the denizens of the Earth to arise in their glorious regalia and glow the light of their love, adoration, and trust for Jesus and the entire Celestial sovereignty of Zion.

You are a royal priesthood, a chosen generation, a holy nation and God's beloved. You are not a subscriber of sorrow, pain, and anxieties because you are a child of light and radiant of God's grace.

THE LIGHT OF THE WORLD

"Never at any stage forget the fact that you are the light of the world, and, in Jesus, you were made such." —Stephen Edoh.

Light is outstanding! It is beautiful, nice and appreciable. Have you at any stage come across a certain bulb with the capacity of emitting light of diverse colour at a time? Yes, is likely to be your answer. I do believe that you felt happy and okay witnessing such a beautiful scene. But the fascinating thing here is this; you are the light of the world and a city on the hilltop; these are the very sayings Jesus is translating in your life at the moment from the frontiers of Zion. Cheers!

Life without light is the same as a car without gasoline or its battery. The journey of life needs the aid of the true light to become an actuality. Until you become a shining light, everything around you trudges in darkness. Feeling sad about an incident is normal, but when it goes beyond the normal duration, it becomes erratic. Whenever we see ourselves as the light of the world, it does not just make us aware of who we truly are but calls for a translation of total subjugation and influence.

The struggles of a man are his privacy, but that of a woman affects the lives within her axis. As a lady or woman of honour and that with differences, you must concord with the fact that your journey in the series of life will only end on a positive note, the very moment you realised your true identity as the light of the world.

When Jesus made you the true light, He wasn't contemplating or guessing whether you deserved to be called the light of the world. He called you because you are His own; you are the replica of His appearance; you display His character everywhere you go, and of all, you love Him. Keep calm, soar!

DEPRESSION

"One thing kills the hope and dreams of our life, unfortunately, it is called depression," —Stephen Edoh

Depression is defined by the Merriam Webster's dictionary, as a state of feeling sad; also it could arise from a medical condition that gave advent to certain emotions detailed by hopelessness, unhappiness, anguish, sorrow, etc. It is also a state that defines the inability of an individual to live a normal life due to one reason or the other clouded by thoughts of negativism.

When you allow anxieties and pains of the past and that of the present to govern your life, then you are under the influence of depression. Depression is not just an enemy of revelation in my first book titled, "A New Dawn", it is the killer of beautiful life stories and visions. Any life that operates under the hegemony of depression suffers the reward of litigations in the series of life.

We live in a time and season when the occurrences of life persuade many people into the state of depression. Unfortunately, it is a strategy imposed by the devil to destroy man and his glorious destiny. Many young people have become a victim of this asshole called, 'depression'; some have felled into it soup due to their inability to sustain admission to the University, get married, etc.

Depression is the catalyst that provokes deceleration in the life of an individual. Any individual under the influence of depression hardly grow or advance, rather such a fellow downshift in the tale of life. The sure and true way is to smile and remain steadfast in the faith, then watch how God turns your captivity around for good. Until the whirlwind of depression is relinquished, growth and advancement seized from taking effect in the life of an individual, team, etc.

I don't know what your dilemmas and situations seem to look like; it could be the inability to source a husband, get an admission into the tertiary institution, poverty, etc. But I tell you the truth, your story is about to change for the better. Jesus is already on your matters, don't give up, don't give in to depression, for your time of laughing has come because laughter is an attribute of a woman of honour.

SMILE

"Your capacity to smile is an effect of God's blessings in your life," – Stephen Edoh

Smiling is the act of an individual or a being in the tale of existence to surface a beautiful and blissful appearance on the face. It is the display of happiness, joy, peace and delight pioneered from the inner mind of an entity. It isn't just the display of happiness, joy, peace and delight, but the translation of God's blessings into reality via the face of an individual or a being. I used the word, 'being' here because not only humans smile, animals do smile; Dogs smiles!

We cannot overemphasise the dynamics of a smile. It is the smartest formula of every woman of honour, a culture in the city of Zion, and an antidote for depression and several emotional ailments in the series of life. In the dealings of life, not every weapon is used in retaliating back to our antagonists. No! Some are specifically designed to fulfil the desired result of the user or operator. So is the same as the act of smiling. It is a mighty arsenal used in the battles fought in the emotional phase of life.

Furthermore, it is the act of conveying a delightful message via a spectacular impression on the face of an individual. It's the network that brings about human connection with happiness and joy. In its absence, the life of a man crumbles. "When we smile, we code the present and the future with joy and delight."

Smiling is a remedy act proposed by many scientists; physiotherapists, physiologist's, etc., around the world. It brings about relief in an awful and turbulent moment. At most times when we smile, it recalls to us on how glorious is our future. Smiling isn't just a remedy. It is a mystery!

When a woman of honour smiles, all you discern is the glory. It makes her appears dazzling and beautiful in the sight of men and too, God. The state of melancholy have so many formulas but 'smile' govern them all. To stay calm in an inopportune moment is good, but smiling while exercising patience is much better.

Our problems are the stepping stones to the hallway of our breakthrough. Each time we smile in the travail, we remind the devil of our impending victory certified by the blood of Jesus. Every woman of honour under-stands this virtue–smile. I know you experienced a situation whereby you were mocked by people who hate you, and you just threw a smile at them. If I might ask, how did they react? Odd, I know, is your answer.

When the devil comes around to mock our weakness, it's up to us to remind him of our strength by smiling. We display an attitude of strength and bravery each time we smile, and the devil stumbles afterwards. The magnitude of our travails isn't bigger than the size of the God we serve It's a shame for you to believe that the devil has defeated you completely. Common, get up! It's time you glance at him with a smile to provoke his jealousy and state of unrest.

The act of smiling triggers the increase in the life span of a man. People who smiles don't die young. They kill their problems before it annihilates them. Anywhere depression, anxiety, sin, worries are absent, you can't hear of death taking hold of such a territory. It is to the pioneer of optimism and sanguinity displayed by an individual, family, or a team.

Smiling is a gift you must value. It is the balm of life; rub it on your face daily. Too, it's the ruby and emerald that glance at your beauty, value them. It is the language of Zion speak them. Never forsake this beautiful mystery the delightful Celestial king deposited into your life. It is a means to bring glory to His holy name. Always appreciate Him; for He is the King of all kings, and God over gods. He's the one Baal and Dagon bow to, the one who created the entire universe, the extraordinary Man of war, and finally, the great Kadosh.

Stay with me!

Vision

" **E**very woman or lady you have encountered in the journey of life admires the position and places of influence." —Stephen Edoh.

Vision is a plain snapshot of our plans, passions, aspirations, yearnings, goals, etc. I would like to recite a quote from my first book, titled: A New Dawn, "Life without vision, operate in friction." In the series of life, the essential and crucial key to explore any horizon is a vision.

The word, 'Vision' could be linked to constructing a foundation; which then detail the fact that the vision of every woman is the bedrock of her future. It is the lens of success that views our imagination, opens us to our aspiration, and steers us to the hallway of honour.

Often, many people say they want to be admired, famous, rich etc. But the lost key which they still do not have access to is a vision. When you lack a vision for something, you can't envision or dream of anything encouraging, because vision brings out the blueprint of your future as a woman of honour.

Most ladies out there are not making an impact, not because they are ungodly, or odd. No! They aren't visionary. Until a woman becomes prescient, her home remains a mundane empire. Yet, she and her husband might be rich and healthy, but still, not amplifying impact to the denizens of the earth.

Historically, the success of several distinguished intellectuals materialises via the influence of visionary women in their life. Such nobles include Zondervan's own Dr Ben Carson, whose momma influence and faith trigger his dream of becoming a neurosurgeon. Also, women such as Faith Oyedepo, Becky Enenche, Judith Edoh play an outstanding role in their husband's success.

Vision is a platform that built the aspiration of every woman to the hilltop. It introduces the passion and zeal for success. Life outside vision is life inside tension. This is the reason a lot of ladies goes into prostitution; because they didn't have an obvious sight of who they are. So, they ended up in a state of tension.

I groaned in pain the very moment I realised most ladies are living to fulfil the demand for reproduction and sexual satisfaction. But the story is beyond! God didn't ordain any intimacy from the throne room for alone the purpose of reproduction and sexual pleasure, but to translate impactful feats in the tale of mankind. This is the reason most homes are blossoming; because the couples are visionary.

We have sailed down this far; still, we have to explore more on this series.

A GODLY HOME

"One of the topmost primacies of any lady or woman is that of creating a space for a godly atmosphere in her home." —Stephen Edoh.

Godliness is the translation of the divine spirit that legislate from the hamlet of Zion. It is the God kind of personality; the ways He loves, the culture he held in awe, etc. In a time when the whirlwind of civilization seems to act hostile to the denizens of the earth, only the godly individuals stand firm!

Many people used to think of the Godly sets of people as abnormal and erratic fellows with no hope. But it's not true!

Godliness is the foundation of every vision that denote the triggering power of Jesus Christ. In godliness one find peace and joy, otherwise, it shows up from a different side; mundane activities, etc. Any move embarked on the backing of godliness stride on to the doorway of honour. Every vessel of honour you know of is a caption of a godly heritage.

The first goal of every female entity either in courtship or in marriage must be based on its targets on the fact of raising a godly home. Men don't raise the home, they built a house. Women are home builders! Still, they can be home destroyers at the same time. But the fact here is this; as a woman or a lady, your first target must be that of raising a godly home.

A godly home is not the same as the regular homes we do visit time after time. No! It differs. It's a home that housed God's favour in all virtues. The Celestial present never finds its route to an ungodly home for any reason. It only recognises the righteous and that of the just.

The benefits of raising an excellent home translated not only for a vision that positively affects the life and wellbeing of a single-family. No! It influence affect the entire universe. Dr Benjamin Carson isn't great today because he was handsome, rich, or intelligent. No! He is because a godly woman stood in the gap for him when he was a no-brainer. Today, the entire world celebrates both Benjamin and Sonya Carson.

When a woman submits her home to Jesus, she submits a part of the nation's population to the host of heaven. Just imagine for once every woman raising godly children for the next 20yrs. You will find out that the crime rate will be at the point of eradication. The world will be a lovely place for everyone to live in. Never forget, the influence of a godly activity spread so far like the wide fire.

Finally, God's love for the righteous can't be outclassed by anyone; even the Biblical psalmists testify in most of their melodies of God's involvement in safeguarding the righteous.

Remember, others might put their trust in chariots and horses, but a godly woman or lady relies on the true God. It's a prime time you put up with the right decision by agreeing at this very moment that you will raise a godly home, not just with yourself but with God.

Stay with me!

IMPACT

"One of those things that make several women more unique than most men is the tale of impact."—Stephen Edoh.

Impact is the effect that translates from the lifestyle or the personality of an entity being referred to as the encoder or the mentor to the individual in reference; the mentee or the decoder. It is the transmission of abstract thought, feelings, ways of life, etc., from one person to another.

The impact could neither be negative kind; changing men into monsters or a positive kind; influencing, converting and sending men and women to their place of destiny.

The lamp of every man's education shines so brightly. But that of a woman shine brighter. Every impact made by a woman transform the beings around her region. A famous quote says, "If you educate a man, you have taught one person, but when you educate a woman, you enlighten the society." This only happens via impact!

One difference that makes a woman appreciable is an impact. Many people are out there but nobody appreciates or value them because they haven't impacted something excellent into the life of anyone. Until you arose to become a factor of celebration, the world wouldn't acknowledge your presence on the Earth surface.

Women of honour are the very dimensions and portals of impact. As soon as an individual or team's of persons encountered a woman of tremendous impact, their life changes for good. You can't meet with an entity such as Kathryn Kuhlman and remain the same. No! This is a custodian; one who legislates as a kingdom remnant.

Many people complain about certain factors that contribute to one being impactful and the formal criterion been given is based on financial capability; riches. But this is never true. The impact is not for the rich alone. It is less for everyone to become a man and woman of impact. This is because it pays not a family alone but the entire society.

Women of impact are those who aid their husbands in raising a godly home. Remember, I earlier said something to be taken note of, "Every ungodly home is a profane dynasty ." Yeah, it is true, because when God spirit is absent from home, a strange Spirit takes refuge in such a cottage. Never forget, a godly home is a citadel where Kingdom remnants are erected.

Impact defines a woman as a component of honorarium when such a woman cultivates an attitude of teaching and fostering wonderful insights into the life of several persons out there. When you come across a family whose mental and emotional state is at equilibrium, what then comes to your mind is the fascinating personality of the custodian of that home; such in reference is the mother.

Finally, a woman of impact is one who has discovered her calling. Not just the fact of realising whom God had called her to be on the earth surface but to interpret the purpose of her calling to the inhabitants of the earth by solving critical problems. Women such as Maria Woodworth-Etter and Kathryn Kuhlman are an excellent example of feminists who translated the rhythm of Zion on the Earth surface.

Never forget, the topmost vision of every woman desiring to be named in the hall of fame must be that of raising a godly home and add impact to the life of countless persons out there in the entire universe. Raising a godly home implies building an empire that will help facilitate the movement of the end-time revival. Impact detail a move that will shift the lifestyle of civilization and secularism out of the Earth and positioned godliness on the throne.

Honour

"Every carrier of God's grace is a vessel that expresses honour," —Stephen Edoh.

Honour is an act that translates from an attitude that connotes, love, integrity, appreciation, and indebtedness. God expresses his delightfulness, generosity, and benevolence in the tale of mankind via honour. Man is a product of God's mercy and honour. Daily as the times and seasons of life passed by, one essential factor refers to as, "honour" plays a vast and vital role in the destinies of men.

In the tale of existence, honour speaks, act, and pave the way for us into our glorious destiny. Brilliant men in the Biblical era such as Abraham, Isaac, Daniel, David, and Josiah stood to be a portrait of honour. Others in this chamber include Enoch, Samuel, Anna, Rahab, Ruth, and Jesus Christ. The actualisation of honour is an anecdote that springs forth good consequences.

We would only survive and blossom in this ever trembling world, the moment we propose to operate in the policy of honouring people, and the constitution that governs a territory. But an exception to this, we alter the struggles of our life in a continuous motion as we perished in this spherical part of creation known as the planet Earth.

Unfortunately, many have failed in the various aspects of life. Because their life omits the nature of altruism espoused by honour. The facts we've laid can not decipher the tangibility of honour so far in this series. To further bring this series to a point of elucidation, we have to navigate into an additional dimension for the secrets of honour to become Crystal clear to our comprehending faculty.

Stay with me!

MEEKNESS

"Only the meek individuals can have access to the profound things of God." — Stephen Edoh.

Meekness is the display of a character that evolved from the influence of love, joviality, and mirthfulness. It is the resultant effect of an aura that ensued from a delightful virtue. Still, it translates as a formula that governs the life span of man. Unfortunately, it's one of the noble factor missing in the life of many people.

Pride is the opposite of meekness. It is crystal clear of the fact that God hates proud individuals and honour the modest ones. Pride is a destiny killer! No woman ever live and strives to become an element of honorarium under the influence of pride. Pride is an invisible mechanism that shortens the life span of men on Earth.

Meekness is the character identity of every woman of honour. While pride is the behavioural inscription of a typical mundane woman. Meekness triggers honour, pride catalyst, infamy nor downfall. An excellent example of women whose life detail meekness, include distinguished nobles such as Mother Teresa, Maria Woodworth—Etter, Faith Oyedepo, Sonia Carson, and many much more.

When a woman or a lady operates under the influence or the subjugation of pride, destruction becomes her reward. At most times, we wondered why some ladies are unmarried, but then our inadequacy of knowledge pushes us to ignore the fact of meekness.

Most ladies are still spinster today, not because the Mr Right meant for them hasn't shown up, but because pride glows in every aspect of their life. Until you shut down pride; your life keeps roaming about an orbit of complexity. Every woman has a decision, but one of the best she can make is to be meek!

GRATITUDE

"The influence of gratitude is beyond the dealings of a typical man's realm,"—Stephen Edoh.

Gratitude is an act that emerged from the impact of appreciation, fondness, acknowledgement, and honour. Otherwise, it is the culture of exhibiting concern about a positively triggered occurrence. As much as many have a chosen to skip this word, "gratitude", God will continue to skip them.

Ingratitude is the opposite of gratitude; it conveys an expression of thanklessness, ungratefulness and unappreciation. Ingratitude is a negative catalyst! It slows down the progress of many people. Also, it destroys intimacy between two or more people.

There were ten lepers in the Biblical days of Jesus who got healed from the malady of leprosy. But guess what? Only one of them returned to express his gratitude, and Jesus perfected his healing. Ingratitude triggers imperfection in the handiwork of God, in the tale of humanity. While gratitude pioneers perfection upon the move of God in the series of life.

When you learn to appreciate and show gratefulness to people upon every impact they made on your life, God learns to bless you continuously. The reasons most women are enjoying a home of solace today is because they adopted the spirit of gratefulness and appreciation. The absent of ingratitude in a home or a relationship triggers a poor communication between the partners.

Every lady and woman of honour must adopt the spirit of fondness and gratefulness because it is one secret that transforms a home to a mighty castle. Praying to God for a change of attitude and consistent renewal of the mind can bring about the embracing of gratefulness. One wonderful fact stands still; gratitude is a character component that expresses honour.

IMPARTIALITY

"The Holy Spirit was an outstanding example of a being whose expressions denote impartiality," — Stephen Edoh.

Impartiality is the culture of showing equality in terms of treatment, works routine, leadership in the affairs of life. It is the effect that translates from a spirit that legislates in the city of Zion. Impartiality is the pioneer of the growth and progress in developed nations today.

One of the major problem faced by the labour force of every nation took effect because of expulsion smashed on the countenance of impartiality. Today, in most organisation, industries and even the church it is difficult to get a job, not because there is no vacancy, but because of the effect of corruption.

Our world is trembling today because of partiality from the times of old. The Biblical patriarch Jacob was one of those who brought about the tradition and lifestyle of partiality; when he lavish love for Joseph than the others of his brothers, and this in return birthed hatred towards Joseph from his brothers.

Partiality is the foundation of failure and the bedrock of underdevelopment in many corrupt nations. It is the pioneer of nepotism and a high ranking soldier in the armies of corruption. Every dream built on the platform of partiality ends in destruction. Partiality is a hindrance to an evergreen world.

Unfortunately, most mothers and even ladies display an odd attitude by conveying partiality in their family affairs; treating one child better, favouring one than the other. It's all bad! As a woman or a lady who aim at being a factor of honorarium, the lifestyle of partiality must be excluded from your thoughts and reasoning faculty.

When you learn to treat everyone equally, hatred and strife shifts from afar. The reason Joseph brothers couldn't contend with their hatred other than the surface it was because their father refused to change his attitude towards them. You must learn to treat people equally because it is a virtue of honour.

Negligence to all you have read in this series will leave you with nothing but shame! Never forget the fact that you are God's own apple; so, it is up to you to please Him by displaying an attitude that translates for good and honour, and that which brings glory to God.

About the Author

Edoh Stephen Owoicho was born in Plateau State, Nigeria to a Benue indigent parents in the year, 1999. He grew up in New Karu, Nasarawa State, Nigeria. For six years he has been writing poems, articles, and songs. His first book, "A New Dawn," earn a recommendation, from many Nigerians and friends abroad. In 2019, he wrote his second book, "Woman of Honour, " which has turned out to be a blessing to many ladies in Africa and beyond.

Furthermore, He is a medical physiology student at the prestigious College of Health Sciences, Benue State University, Nigeria. Also, He is the founder of Words Citadel Family; a spoken and written team who's goal is to stir, inspire and transform the lost and broken.

Stay with Edoh Stephen Owoicho

Also by Edoh Stephen Owoicho

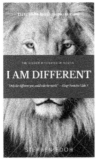

I am Different

An Evergreen World

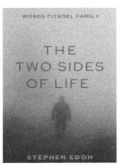

The two Sides of Life

A new Dawn

Lightning Source UK Ltd.
Milton Keynes UK
UKHW010630220721
387590UK00001B/115